COMPUNDIUM

1001 puns to read before you die. Weed 'em and reap.

Robert Laidler And Mark Harvey

**Copyright © 2024 Robert Laidler And Mark Harvey **

All rights reserved. No part of this book may be reproduced, distributed, or transmitted in any form or by any means, including photocopying, recording, or other electronic or mechanical methods, without the prior written permission of the publisher, except in the case of brief quotations embodied in critical reviews and certain other non-commercial uses permitted by copyright law. For permission requests, please contact the publisher at the address below.

This is a work of fiction. Names, characters, businesses, places, events, and incidents are either the products of the author's imagination or used in a fictitious manner. Any resemblance to actual persons, living or dead, or actual events is purely coincidental.

If bees live in an apiary, where do apes live?...

"Proud pals produce a proper premier, pantheon of punnery."

***** The Daily Alliteration

"Compundium: a veritable Selection Box of one-liners without the chocolate."

***** Placebo Domingo, The Fake Tenor

"Yet more blunt edged comedy from this pair of Clackmannanshire crackpots."

* The Menstrie Mercury

"There're puns here for everyone and should be seen, read and heard everywhere. You could say, they put the I, U and US into ubiquitous."

***** The Widespread News Channel.

"This book is a reel catch—you'll be hooked from the first page!"

**** Carmarthenshire Angler's Quarterly

"Reading this was a piece of cake, and you butter believe it's hilarious!"

***** Stoneybridge Baker's Bugle**

"I was pawsitively glued to the pages—this book is the cat's whiskers!"

***** Aberdeen Cat Fanciers Monthly**

"Prepare to be blown away—this book is a real pun-ami of laughter!"

***** The Official Michael Fish Fan Club**

COMPUNDIUM.

1001 puns to read before you die.

Weed 'em and reap.

When Hawkeye Brown met Joss of Alva... Scenes from the Mar Café.

I reckon that it's the dampness that dominates our weather that gifts us Scots with our unique sense

of humour. In a bid to fend off the discomfort, we make our voices heard.

Back in 1986 Mark (Hawkeye Brown) and Robert (Joss of Alva) sat in Alloa's Mar Café, sharing a cup

of tea and a square sausage roll, wondering why on earth we'd chosen this route out of, what was

referred to as, a Comprehensive education. It quickly became a meeting of like minds that was to

spawn a life-long journey through nonsense and non-conformity.

With degrees in reverse psychology and backward thinking, plus non-stop puntificating about this crazy life, we opened a giant can of Scottish words together, and in 1986 Jockney Rhyming Slang was created, it was just the start.

Remaining firmly under the radar, hiding in plain sight, secretly causing pundemoneum along the

way, we created a body of work that would eventually become the Compundium that you are about to dip into ….let the pun begin.

If you enjoy our book, then why not check out more puns at our website, www.compundium.com, or scan the QR code below.

CONTENTS

ART	14
Joss	14
Hawkeye	15
BUSINESS	17
Joss	17
Hawkeye	24
CHARITY	28
Joss	28
Hawkeye	29
CHRISTMAS	30
Joss	30
Hawkeye	31
CONFLICT	32
Joss	32
Hawkeye	36
CRIME	37
Joss	37
Hawkeye	40
EDUCATION	42
Joss	42
Hawkeye	45
FAMILY	47
Joss	47
Hawkeye	49

FASHION	51
Joss	51
Hawkeye	52
FILMS	53
Joss	53
Hawkeye	55
FOOD AND DRINK	60
Joss	60
Hawkeye	64
FRANCE	71
Joss	71
Hawkeye	73
GARDENING	74
Joss	74
Hawkeye	75
GREAT BRITISH TOWNS	78
Joss	78
Hawkeye	81
HEALTH	82
Joss	82
Hawkeye	83
HISTORY	84
Joss	84
Hawkeye	85
HOBBIES	87

Joss	87
Hawkeye	90
HOME	93
Joss	93
Hawkeye	95
LITERATURE	96
Joss	96
Hawkeye	98
MEDICAL	99
Joss	99
Hawkeye	103
MUSIC	108
Joss	108
Hawkeye	111
NATURAL WORLD	118
Joss	118
Hawkeye	120
OFFICE	123
Joss	123
Hawkeye	126
PETS	127
Joss	127
Hawkeye	129
PHILOSOPHY	130
Joss	130

Hawkeye	133
POLITICS	**134**
Joss	134
Hawkeye	136
RELATIONSHIPS	**138**
Joss	138
Hawkeye	139
RELIGION	**140**
Joss	140
Hawkeye	142
SCIENCE	**144**
Joss	144
Hawkeye	146
SCOTLAND	**147**
Joss	147
Hawkeye	148
SOCIAL MEDIA	**149**
Joss	149
Hawkeye	150
SPORT	**151**
Joss	151
Hawkeye	156
STORIES	**164**
Hawkeye	164
SUPERNATURAL	**168**

Joss	168
Hawkeye	169
TRAVEL	**170**
Joss	170
Hawkeye	174
TV	**177**
Joss	177
Hawkeye	178
WORDS	**183**
Joss	183
Hawkeye	184
X-RATED	**186**
Joss	186
Hawkeye	189

ART

Joss

Has any artist out there actually drawn a blank?

Is the writing finally on the wall for rogue graffiti artists?

Piss artist finally wins Turner Prize with urine sample.

They tell me that people who work in art galleries are more likely to have hang ups about their job than any other profession.

Back to the drawing board can make drawing very difficult.

Hawkeye

It's now been 12 months trying to find out who was the original owner of a French antique painting I bought. It's been a year in provenance.

I always thought the Belgian, surrealist artist, Magritte, was just some Scottish wuman.

Remnant : the last of the great Dutch painters.

UN street artist comes to town: Banksie Moon.

Details of a local artist's attempted robbery of a paint shop remain sketchy.

Feeling arty so cut out bits of paper from The Sun, Herald, Scotsman and Guardian and made a giant papier mâché figure. It's mixed media.

BUSINESS

Joss

Consumerism will eat itself.

Do they hold "all staff" events for walking stick manufacturers?

I once knew an ingenious entrepreneur who was arrested for setting up a pyramid selling scheme in Egypt.

Is there any truth in the rumour that Fairtrade producers favour Albino employees?

For years I thought a crib sheet was a baby's blanket.

A General is ranked higher than a Captain yet it's always the General Dogsbodies who end up having to take orders from the Captains' of Industry.

The digital revolution, is it simply just a huge wind up?

Perhaps J Edgar Hoover should have investigated this one. If a vacuum is "a space totally devoid of all matter" why on earth did man have to invent a device to clean it?

Wannabe Albino accused of blond ambition.

The other day I noticed an advert in a jeweller's window for a vintage gents watch. Confusingly, they described it as a "timeless classic".

I once knew a hypnotist who was so good at what he did that he actually failed as even his own business went under.

Yesterday I had to read twice the sign in the window of a clothing alterations shop. Amazingly, it was claiming to offer the customer a "seamless service" from start to finish.

My watch appears to be broken, can anyone out there give me the number of a decent, time served horologist?

Barter, it's the way forward and it tastes much better than breadcrumbs.

Can anyone tell me how much has the free market cost us?

Despite the media fuelling speculation that petrol and diesel prices are set to come down at the pumps, I suspect that the major oil companies will always have us over a barrel.

When I was employed as a Salesman for a Lift Company, the most awkward part of the job was always the elevator pitch.

I wonder if there will ever be a book titled, "The Complete History of the Futures Markets"?

I recently applied for a Doorman's job, sadly I failed the Entrance Exam.

See the amount of trouble I've had with mail order companies recently. It's been a catalogue of disasters.

If they were handing out prizes for Britain's best Safari Park, it would be really interesting to see if Longleat would make the short leet.

Bench- Marking, is that not just park graffiti?

With fly tipping now at an all time high, now feels like a really profitable time to become an insect.

I was gutted when I landed my job as a High Court Judge, as the Procurator told me it would be on a trial basis only.

When I first started my job as a Toilet Attendant I loved it, but it wasn't long before I was just going through the motions.

I often wonder who changes the bag in the Hoover Dam.

What do you put on the front of a Back Catalogue?

The best task I was ever handed, when working in advertising, was to come up with a strap line for a leading bra manufacturer.

Yesterday I swear I overheard an Estate Agent on the phone saying to his client "Have I got mews for you?"

I hear that there is a co-operative in Castlemilk who have got together to open a new French/Spanish restaurant, they've named it Chateaux Olé.

Midwifery: The most labour intensive job in the world.

Be careful. Starting up your own funeral business can be a huge under-taking.

Even though I've been voted Scotland's top colander designer for six years in a row now, my boss still picks holes in my work.

Over two hundred butchers face the chop in a carve up of the meat industry.

Badge making giants pin hopes on a new sew on solution.

Shock as boss of Canon is fired in boardroom battle.

Man sacked as boss points out 144 examples of gross misconduct.

Wheel making industry leaders say re-invention is inevitable as they've been going round in circles for too long.

I remember the days when the skyscraper business was little more than a cottage industry

I hear that the jetty down at our beach has collapsed into the sea, they're blaming it on pier pressure.

Ye Olde Sale – Get your medieval torturing equipment

here……Hurry while stocks last.

Alan Fresco – Interior Designer "Bringing the Outside In"

Cisterns Development - 21st Century plumbing

When Britain goes fully digital in a few years time I suppose it will mean the end of aerial photography.

Dorothycom.com the original Dot.com

Knife manufacturers slash prices in factory ticketing carnage.

Isn't it odd that Convenience Stores never seem to stock new toilets?

Hawkeye

Had a very mixed experience at my local supermarket. One minute, the checkout girl was being nice to me, the next, she was shouting at me...it really was good co-op, bad co-op.

Got some great shoe bargains in a retail factory, near Sellafield. Was served by a lovely assistant at the Kurt Geiger counter.

My son is always on my back for money so I gave him a piggy-bank ride.

Edinburgh's investment area is located between Stockbridge and Grassmarket.

Wursprung Doon Teesnik, as they say in Newcastle.

The tennis player, Juan Carlos Ferrero, and the Irish football player, Stephanie Roche, have sent the ambassador a box of chocolates.

Meerkats insurance must, ironically, be quite expensive, seeing as there's no doors or windows in their burrows.

Owner of candle company admits to burnout and says his staff were getting on his bloody wick.

The only market research poll that I love is the Amore poll.

Do you ever get emergency entrances?

If there is a tax on tacks, would carpetbaggers have to pay?

The Dow Jones was originally a livestock market in Wales.

A fizzy drinks company was today put into liquidation. Workers claim that management bottled it.

St Trademark is the Patent Saint of Copyright.

He was the President of the National Union Of Mineworkers, back in the 80's, and to many, he was a snail in the grass. That was Arthur L'Escargill.

I love my Ironmongrels; he can mix and match almost anything.

I take it Spanish fishermen use castanets.

The textile community is a close knit world.

Going at it hammer and tongs with my new bakery business. I'm all buns glazing.

These French baggage handlers are so slow. L'escargo.

Roofers love to get the big jobs obviously, but it's the small ones that are their lead and gutter.

Was the King's plumber corgi registered, I wonder?

A factory which makes light bulbs had a complete change of mind this week when a proposed plan to open a new factory was put on the shelf. They apologised for this volt-farce.

An anagram is just a managar who can't spell.

I'm making a fortune from alternative medicine: I'm reiking it in.

HUGE queue waiting to get into the glass recycling depot. It was a real bottleneck.

CHARITY

Joss

My close friend the Funky Nomad tells me that the RAF are planning a massive charity airshow in Fife for retired pilots. If the idea ever gets off the ground they're going to call it Leuchars Aid.

A WI member turns to her friend and says "Watch out, it's a jumble out there."

I'm quite pleased with myself, I've managed to set up my new Excema Charity completely from scratch.

Charities, I think I've heard it all now "Decembeard". Mind you, at least the ladies can get involved in this one.

Hawkeye

Currently dyeing my beard purple for Mauvember.

Narcissistic philanthropist admits showering himself with praise over a 3 year period.

The new thing at this time of year is MOTember, where you let your bushes grow for a month.

CHRISTMAS

Joss

As a Christmas treat a farmer gave his sheep some boiled sweets and all they could say in return was baa humbug.

Wassail of the Century. Christmas bargains.

Hawkeye

Going to have a socially distanced Christmas meal this year by having it in a tent in the back garden. Got everything in apart from the pegs and blankets.

At Christmas, you surely never expect things to go smoothly with kids. That's where the naivety play comes in.

I'm thinking of writing a yuleogy about the death of Xmas and it's over commercialism.

St Nicholas has a claus in his contract for a statutory week's holiday, starting 26th December each year.

CONFLICT

Joss

Hundreds of villagers have their noses blown off as Cold War brings Russia to it's sneeze.

Bush blamed for yet another fatality as War of the Roses escalates.

Hundreds of wild pigs slaughtered as fighting in the Boar War continues.

Great Bear killed by Plough as star wars escalate.

Baker in hospital following bun fight at the Oatcake Corral

Aggrophobia – the fear of fighting

Bush blamed for yet another fatality as fighting intensifies in war of the roses.

If people would just give up fighting for peace there would be no more wars.

Food fights - a war of nutrition

No quarter is ever given or asked between warring fractions.

Man killed by freezer as Cold War escalates.

Three silverbacks have been killed as fighting between Gorilla factions rage on in Borneo.

Hundreds of fish die as cod war continues.

A team of Jam Doughnuts fought off the challenge of the French Fancies to win the inaugural World Bun Fighting Championships in Bakersville Masc USA. A spokesman for the Doughnuts told reporters that "the victory hadn't exactly been a cake walk, however, it was definitely their Bakerloo.

Man grassed in city pub as turf wars spill into built up areas.

Inn fighting continues as the Black Bull knocks out the Red Lion after fifteen rounds.

Hundreds killed in Axeminster as carpet bombing continues.

Primate of all England killed as gorilla warfare continues.

Man freezes to death in cold war battle.

Ten men mowed down mercilessly in turf war battle.

Man bored to death during prolonged ceasefire in Boer War.

The only way to stop arguments about money is to make it non denominational.

Intense fighting broke out tonight between rival campanologists at St Swithens Parish Church, Stevenage. Local police described it as a ding dong battle.

The Charge of the Light Brigade, was the cost too high?

Hawkeye

Weapons of mass destruction found at Labyrinth nursing home. Investigators said it was full of nukes and grannies.

I'm surprised The Civil War had any casualties.

I fell off my bike at Waterloo, injured my knee at Culloden and hit my head going round Bannockburn. You could say that I've been in the wars.

I was held hostage for a week and in that time, grew to hate my captor. I had Gothenburg syndrome.

CRIME

Joss

Scotland Yard plumber in "hot water" after tapping allegations.

Just how do criminal lawyers keep on getting away with it?

"Book thrown at Novel Killer" – A writer who slayed his real life victims by pen was finally sentenced to death by Judge Dickens at the Old Bailey. In summing up the Judge added that he was pleased to be bringing a particularly sad chapter to a close.

A black faced ewe has accused Rogue, the border collie of stalking her at a sheep dog trial in the High Court, Harrogate.

Man gets trapped in barrel as he rides shotgun.

Actor escapes after courtroom drama.

Pandamonium - a Police car pile up?

Do the police keep the records of sex offenders in Peado Files?

Benefits cheats in the French capital have been branded parisites by President Macron.

Do forensic scientists carry out detailed examinations of crash scenes using a collidascope?

US prison inmates are seemingly now banned from using mobiles, however it doesn't matter much as they all still have their cell phones.

Real criminals must remain committed at all times.

Murder by shampoo - is usually premedicated.

Could a recurring dream about being put in prison for a while be considered a stretch of the imagination?

Someone sprinkled coconut over a grave in our local cemetery, a Police spokesman described it as the worst case of dessication he'd ever seen.

Most material evidence has been fabricated.

They have a pub in our local open prison. In a bold move to reduce the number of inmates absconding, the Governor has now introduced lock-ins seven nights a week.

Hawkeye

Amberguity. Should you jump the lights or not?

Lettuce thief strikes again but police say that it's only the tip of the iceberg.

Ex-wrestling junkie loses hidden syringe whilst doing community service on a farm. It's like looking for a needle in a giant haystack.

The Government is hoping to build 10 new duplicate prisons around the country, with the help of stem cell research.

The head of MI5 must have a finger in a lot of spies.

I'm gonna blow the lid on body snatchers.

So many different fabrics to choose from for reupholstery before executing someone. It's the eclectic chair.

Salt and vinegar has just shot cheese and onion, swiftly and mercilessly in cold blood: it was a crisp execution.

Monarchy's pet department to sue paper for wrongful neglect claims. Regal beagle eagle legal action to be taken.

Police had to break up rival jeans factory workers today. They said pockets of violence had broken out.

Police investigating the suspicious death of an escapologist, say there are no major leads to follow and that it's a real Houdinit.

Heard the one about the South African highwayman? Rand and de liver.

I bought some toothpaste the other day that gave me total protection. How come I was mugged that night?

EDUCATION

Joss

Having to take a Night Class in English - the sign of a mispelt yoof.

I studied keys at Yale for five years, found my way out then had an on off affair with a girl who worked in the Connecticut switch factory

At school I was pulled up for speaking too fast, I explained to the Head that it was because I'd been taught using the frenetic alphabet.

Yesterday I spotted a swede in our local library, which was a right turnip for the books.

They're talking about banning conkers at school again. Not that old chestnut.

Having been educated at the School of Hard Knocks, it opened many a door for me later on.

Most exam cheats go on to become copywriters.

I loved bookkeeping at school so much that I knew one day I'd become a Librarian.

Most people who join the Navy attended Boarding Schools.

At Drama School we only ever had an acting Headmaster.

Is there any point in doing past papers for Modern Studies?

Anyone out there failed an Acid Test?

I finally passed the bar exam and now I'm an Advocate. Luckily I've secured a job, but it's on a trial basis only.

I've just passed the Foundation Course to become a makeup artist. Totally made up now.

I'm not going to University to become a Hypnotist after all, as I've just failed the Intrance Exam.

Hawkeye

My chemical teacher was the absolute worst at school. He didn't know his arsenic from his erbium.

Doing mental arithmetic, fractions etc leaves me breathless. I think I'm asmathic.

Should it not really be Zero Intolerance?

Illiteracy really isn't anything to write home about.

Two Maths departments are having to reduce their staff numbers at the end of the current term. Professor Tangent said although they were both coefficient, it was just a sine of the times.

My part time algebra teacher died today, so I'm flying my flag at halfmaths.

The irony is, that although the periodic table is usually my speciality, I failed my chemistry exam on the FE question.

There's always two sides to every story; unless you're discussing trigonometry.

Bloody exam board. They got my history and electronic exam dates mixed up. Total histrionics shown by everyone.

Got a degree in microphone skills. I got a 1-2 1-2.

FAMILY

Joss

Relative calm prevails as Scotland's top genealogist brothers finally end family feud over tree.

Genealogy – it's all relative.

When he was a youngster Uri Geller's mum only ever asked him to set the table once

As bakers in the sixties my parents were part of the flour power movement, which meant that I was self raised whereas my sister was plain.

Kidology – the study of young goats.

If necessity is the mother of invention .. who's the daddy?

Parenthesis - Is that the painful transformation that men

and women go through following the birth of their first child?

Hawkeye

Granite: A tough, no nonsense, Aberdeen Granny.

I only really like celebrating the big birthdays, so it was a surprise when I found out that my wife was going to throw me a 39th birthday party for me. You see, it's just not my forte.

My brother- in- law is great at making curtains, but no one believes him. They say it's just a fabrication.

Genealogy: I rubbed a bottle once and out came my grand-father, great-great uncle and my 3rd cousin on my mother's side.

Very proud to announce my son, Paul Junior, is now on the board of our nightwear company.

Have one brother living in Warsaw and another in Krakow. However, you couldn't find 2 more different people. They're poles apart.

Kids are just so simile these days. I was like...

Einstein's theory of relativity, originally was about his uncles, aunts and cousins.

FASHION

Joss

Former DJ turned zip magnate YKK, finally hailed as "Lord of the Flies"

Kelvin Clyde - Glasgow's fashionista

I was just wondering if fatigues make you more tired than when you wear standard military gear?

I remember when donkey jackets used to cost hee haw.

They say that we live in a material world, yet it's so hard to find a decent bit of cloth these days.

Hawkeye

Thinking of shaving off that awful 90s haircut? Mullet over before you do anything hasty.

Monochrome is the new black.

I don't care much for the FCUK clothing range. I'm more into SHTI (Sainsbury's Homebase Training Institute)

Does Claudia Schiffer ever wear a Wunderbra?

Daft twins open fabric shops in Harris: Tweedledee and Tweedledum.

FILMS

Joss

New movie based on the lives of infamous Scottish gangland twins…..The MacRaes.

Brief Encounter - what a load of old black and white pants.

They shoot films, don't they?

Odd how there are so few Cowboys and Indians in a Western society.

I struggled with the sub plot in Das Boot.

Simon Pegg visits B&Q. Is this the Dawn of the Shed?

Albino Marciano – The Great White Hope.

Disney's Albino version of Dumbo proves to be nothing more than a white elephant.

Hawkeye

There's an elephant in the room. Dumbo, upon hearing that his father had an affair.

Robert Redford must have been exhausted talking to Desert Orchid and his pals in the film. No wonder it was called the Hoarse Whisperer.

I was on holiday with Quentin Tarantino in Amsterdam recently and as we turned a corner were faced with 6 men in suits. It was a case of Reservoir Clogs and they were all Mr Orange.

Was The Birds part of a Trillogy?

Lucifer is so dramatic, don't you think? The Devil Wears Rada.

Was Alec Guinness a pint sized actor?

A heartwarming story, of how one man overcame a

speech impediment, to help thousands of others. Schindler's Lisp.

I hear Jennifer Aniston is to appear as a software programmer, in a new film, with the inevitable love interest thrown in. It's a CD Rom-Com.

Star Wars Outtakes. May The Farce Be With you.

It is so easy to get tunnel vision by eating the same meat all the time. Try to escape the monotony by mixing it up . The Ham Shank Redemption.

If you keep turning Stanley Kubrick's name, you eventually get The Rubik's Cube.

Silence Of The Lambs: Shear tension.

My favourite animal in Star Wars was the Lightsaber Tooth Tiger.

I copied Blackbeard the movie for some friends, but was convicted of piracy.

Put a Tolkien in the slot and you'll dial M for Mordor.

Jack Nicholson playing golf would surely be, One Flew Over the Putting Green.

The Marx brothers were also known as Tomfoolery, Dickfoolery and Harryfoolery.

Was Charlton Heston good at the Charleston?

Saw a lovely teenage growing up story set 10,000 years ago. It was a coming-of ice age-film.

Austin-tatious Powers...what a showoff.

Pinocchio puts all his wood shavings into the chiminea cricket.

License to pay: James Bond at the Post Office, renewing his car tax for the Aston Martin.

50 grains of shale : a geologist's dirty weekend.

Loved the movie, Salmon Fishing in the Yemen. It had so many top actors in it. I suppose you could say, it had a great cast.

I like to think Ferrous Bueller could have appeared in Ironman.

Lost my bloody ring under the fridge. Now I'm going to have to dismantle the whole thing to find it. It'll be the desolation of Smeg.

The surprising role Newcastle volunteers played in Vietnam: Platoon Army.

Also dealing with the after effects on hearing that Newcastle narrowly lost out on the Premier league title: Full Mental Straight Jacket.

Julia Roberts' new film is a strange choice about the workings of the bowel and all its intricacies. It's called sleeping with the enema.

Rumours that John Travolta and Samuel L Jackson were refused entry to a juice bar in L.A were completely untrue. It was just pulp fiction.

Can't wait to see The Dark Knight Rises: Garry Kasparov was always a hero of mine.

The Cannibal Run: it's a dog eat dog world out there in Hollywood.

Arnold Schwarzeneggar's new film, The Procrastinator, is due to open this Friday. His new catchphrase no doubt will start doing the rounds. I'll be back...maybe next week sometime.

FOOD AND DRINK

Joss

Soup making - still just a potage industry

Thyme finally runs out for Britain's oldest herb sage Rosemary Dill, aged 90. She later said "I've never let my stock dwindle before!"

Arithmetical genius nonplussed by poor quality takeaway in Bearsden.

All top bread makers really need to know is to know how to knead.

Fizzyology - the study of carbonated drinks.

I was once a stakeholder in the world's biggest vegetarian company.

Sandwiches can never be real as they are always made up by someone.

Is it possible to get whole foods in half portions or would the description change?

Where does Concentrate come from? I just wondered as so many of our drinks and smoothies appear to be made from it.

Seemingly the draft edition of the new Good Beer Guide went down better than the published version.

There's a rumour going around in our workplace that Chinese Wispas taste better than the Scottish ones.

If you were born with a bag of Silver Spoon in your mouth, you probably had a Sugar Daddy.

Can apes eat canapes?

I tried eating a Double Decker the other day but I ran into a bit of trouble …. it got stuck under my bridge.

Hunger pangs: Thought for food.

Is a vegetable garden simply a walled off salad?

You'd have thought that they would have created a smaller tin for condensed milk by now?

Hardest job I ever had was tinning Evaporated Milk.

Do you think they'll ever bring out a Rough Guide to Smoothies?

I was once headhunted for a job as a chef for a tribe of cannibals.

If you ask me, as meats go, Biltong is Pete Tong

Strange how chicken skewers are always made out of wood.

How odd that when you melt black ice into a glass the water is clear.

Can anyone out there think up a good adage for a takeaway?

They say that men who drink draught beer are more prone to wind.

French Toast: Gallic Bread

Laphroaig: Gaelic for Leapfrog

Pan - the God of the Half Loaf.

Hawkeye

Did a wine tasting tour of Scotland recently and my head is bursting: it was a napper valley trip.

I'm absolutely fizzing at not being allowed my customary drink before curtains up. It was only a presecco.

Trying to think of a spice that springs to mind that goes in a variety of cuisines: I suppose something that's cinnamonyus.

I'm all in favour of having custard with alcohol these days. I'd definitely advocate that.

Article on breakfast news about the dangers of snakebites and the number of people dying from them. Well stop drinking so much cider & lager.

Absolutely love haddock, cod, salmon and tuna. I'm an afishionado.

I admit that I'm crap at making tea and coffee. Mea cuppa.

The study of lettuce isn't that complicated really. I mean, it's not exactly rocket science.

You can write a review on all the really bad restaurants on Tripe advisor.

I think my local chip shop owner has a problem. He stacks up all his fish in neat, horizontal rows and goes ballistic if any of them is put out of plaice. He could have COD.

Went to the world championship cheesemaking championships in Amsterdam today. It all started off in Edam square.

I had a sudden notion the other night for a Mars Bar. It was what you would call an ad choc moment.

The trouble with chocolate is that it repeats on me. The trouble with chocolate is that it repeats on me.

My mother's elder sister never quite seems to cook her pasta right through these days. We call her, Auld Auntie.

I'm going to an Allo' Allo' themed fancy dress dance on Saturday night dressed as pastry with some cream and chocolate drizzled over me. The only problem is which chouxs to wear. It is me, L'Eclair.

Piety : Devoted to pies.

I'm forever banging on about my root vegetable beliefs. I've become radishalised.

I'm salivating every time that bell rings and can't wait for the meringue later. It's Pavlova's dog.

Out for a drink and got beer on my beard and my checked shirt. It was a hopster experience.

My late mum has won a posthummus award for the best chickpea recipe.

Pancakes are cooked in Brighton traditionally on Hove Tuesday.

When you're making a cup of coffee and the steam effect sets off a series of other percolators. That's called a Kettleyst.

Sherlock on clearing up a cheese mystery: "Emmental, my dear Watson."

The national dish of Albania is Tiranamisu.

My favourite burger is the unusual Chubby Checker one. It's a beefburger, but with a twist.

My signature dish is PENne pasta and octopus INK drizzled over it.

Had so much cheese over Xmas, I've put on a bit of weight. Just getting feta and feta.

I can turn any liquid into beer, spirits or wine. I'm an alkymist.

Some of my incredibly talented friends have taken to a new reduced sodium flavoured type of crisp. I'm in ex-salted company.

Looking forward to opening up my new venture, The Incendiary Cafe. I'm sure it'll make a bomb.

Fishing levels are at an all time low in the Atlantic. The whitings on the wall.

I use knorrdic stock cubes when making Swedish meatballs.

Bon bon sweets are so good that they named them twice.

I made a beautiful dauphinoise dish at the weekend for friends, but everyone left the room when I brought it out. I was persona non gratin.

A Gallup poll recently showed that people are fed up to the back teeth with the horsemeat scandal.

Missed my job interview at the bakers for head pie maker today. 3.14pm is a stupid time anyway for an appointment.

Immediately gave up sandwiches, soup and twizzlers on Boxing Day. Going cold turkey was hard.

Weightwatchers are trying to be positive but generally failing with their diets. Carpe Dime -seize the chocolate.

IVF cider in deepest Somerset, unfortunately can sometimes take a few goes before the cycle is completed. Or as it's known in the business: Indigenous vernacular fermentation.

Was caught smuggling orange liqueur at the weekend - that's cointreauband for you.

Banana manyana: the leisurely approach to fruit.

Finding evidence of good pub ales isn't easy, but the CAMRA never lies.

Easiest way to get the bill from my Indian/Mediterranean/Middle Eastern restaurant? Just shout out Chick Peas.

Having to make my own bread due to severe lack of funds I'm afraid. Kneads must and all that.

Want to make all that can't make it tonight green with envy? "JUST RAISE A GLASS TO ABSINTHE FRIENDS"

Lebanese vegetables are notoriously difficult to grow as they always show their bare root.

FRANCE

Joss

For years I thought that Bete Noire was french for the song Black Betty by Ram Jam

Coup de grâce - for years I thought that was French for mowing the lawn.

My colleague Kenny thought that the Marquis de Sade was French for a big tent full of fed up people.

Maison d'être: French for bee hive?

When at school I had to translate into English the French words "je suis fatigué". The answer from me was, "I am both fat and gay". The things you come out with!

Creme de Menthe: Cream of the Month

Hawkeye

Jar door. Those French love to leave their portes slightly open.

GARDENING

Joss

That's the trouble with being a gardener, too much ground work.

Confuse your garden designer by asking him, just for once, to come up with an idea in portrait.

My friend Poppy quit her job at the Botanic Gardens yesterday, she finally threw in the trowel.

Hawkeye

Does the four-leaved clover have a square root?

I wanted to get rid of the woodland look and bring in a more Japanese feel to my garden, so it got me thinking, who needs ferns with anemones like these?

My neighbour thinks his grass out the back is pretty special, but all he's done is covered the ground with a weed suppressant. It's mulching dressed as lawn.

Don't underestimate the value of growing your own cabbages. Where there's muck, there's brassicas.

Daffodil war breaks out between rival firms, who are said to be having a real Tete-a-Tete.

Contentment is trying to strike an epimedium

Mahonia has the root of all evil

Lizzie was so busy trying to do everything at once in her garden, she couldn't be bothered persevering with her annual bedding plants. Impatiens is a virtue.

All roads lead to loam.

If I didn't really need to do the pruning before I started to shape my box hedge, is that classed as a non-secateur?

I'm a great fan of donating evergreen shrubs to charities, but never disclose where they come from. I do it euonymus-ly.

It was all a purple haze as the meadow flowers knocked seven bluebells out of each other. They had a violet temper.

Going on an extensive topiary course soon at college. I've been told to think outside the box.

I thought my Dianthus had died last week, but miraculously I nursed it back to health. It was a reincarnation.

Saw a majestic, but slightly erratic, Italian flower display today. The highlight was the Leaning tower of freesia.

The action of pruning your verbena is a verb of course.

So many different types of floral arrangements that I want to try and arrange before I die. I'm going to start a bouquet list.

What's the national flower of New Orleans? Jazzmine of course.

GREAT BRITISH TOWNS

Joss

No matter how hard you try, you'll never please everyone in the town of Umbridge.

The best shopkeeper in the world graduated at Sale College in Trafford.

Tring in Hertfordshire, where the world's first ring tone was heard.

Chard in Somerset, home of the barbeque.

Goring On Sea in West Sussex, bullfighting originated here in the early 16th Century, and Drake sold the idea to the Spanish a few years later.

Woolwich in London, knitted underpants were produced here first.

Grimsdale, the birthplace of Norman Wisdom.

Surrogate in South Yorkshire, my adopted hometown.

Umbridge in Lancashire, the home of the huff.

Evesham in Worcestershire, the town that disproved the book of Genesis.

Sale in Greater Manchester, DFS was founded here 1972.

Poole in Dorset, of course, had the world's first Leisure Centre.

Goole in East Yorkshire, home of Britain's first haunted house.

Andover in Kent. The home of the Relay Race.

Darwen in Lancashire. Where the first seeds of the Theory

of Evolution were first sown.

Hawkeye

Could Axminster in Devon become the first fully carpeted town in the UK?

HEALTH

Joss

Sibling weight loss rivalry has brothers up in arms at frat fighters meeting.

Brain surgeons remain open minded over new lobotomy techniques.

As my Dad once lamented after his failed sex change – " Always the Bridegroom"

Urine samplers were today accused of taking the piss once too often.

Complimentary medicine, how much do you pay for it?

Hawkeye

I have been having acupuncture recently for a bad back, but it's not helping at all. I've found it all rather pointless.

Right, absolutely no more excuses. I've got to give up smoking these cannabis leftover joints. No more spliffs and butts.

Menopause can apparently reduce your sex drive but increase your gas production. That'll be what's known as climax change.

I think Gingers really do get a bad name. Where does that stem from?

I've had four really difficult situations recently: it's been a quadmire.

They don't do nostalgia like they used to.

HISTORY

Joss

I remember the days when the RAF was just a pilot scheme.

Is there any truth in the rumour that Garibaldi was not just a great military leader but also the founder of the Italian Skinhead Movement?

All the finest rulers in the world are made to measure.

It was amazing how people in the Dark Ages just made light of things.

Do really old jokes have hysterical significance?

Hawkeye

The apple never falls far from the tree: Isaac Newton's confused son.

Building Hadrian's Wall was bordering on the ridiculous.

The cleverest and most diverse dinosaur was of course the Thesaurus.

I love these old, romantic French castles, full of historical pieces. I especially liked the suit of amour.

Bobby had no time for spiders whatsoever, and routinely swiped them away. Robert the brusque.

Marco Polo was a real scrooge at Christmas time. He was known as the mint humbug.

William of Normandy on the Bayeux tapestry: They came, they sewed, they conquered.

Went to the Hunterian museum today in Glasgow, but it was full of wellies.

Thought I knew my Egyptian history until I sat my exam. Clearly I didn't revise as I should have. Pharoh nuff I suppose.

Guy Fawkes diary: The Plot Thickens.

Reading the story of Jason and The Argonauts and the journey he was sent on, he was of course completely duped. You could even say he was fleeced.

HOBBIES

Joss

The Domino Theory - you can't knock it

Calligraphy - not so much the font of all knowledge, but the knowledge of all fonts.

When asked recently if he'd seen the steeple at Westminster Abbey, a spokesman for the London Association of Campanologists said that "it didn't ring any bells".

Following the disappearance of German crossword expert Anna Gram. Chief Inspector Wordsworth told reporters that although puzzled they were trying not to get too down and was urging his officers to continue to think inside the box.

The Shepherds accused the Referees of backstabbing at the Annual Whistleblowers Awards last night, but it was the Train Guards who blew away the opposition and picked up the prestigious "Silver Pea".

Rookie Chess champion blames demise on his chequered past.

Isn't it strange that single handed people always seem to be the first to do amazing things ahead of the more able bodied?

I tried fire eating for the first time at the weekend, at one point I had my hearth in my mouth.

The most awkward part of being a Trapeze artist is balancing the easel.

When I was young lad growing up in a
large traditional Circus family I had grate expectations of becoming a fire eater.

Juggling, one of the the few things where making a balls up is acceptable.

If you set up a Free Running Club are you allowed to charge a membership fee?

Petanque: French for bull?

The camaraderie at our Photographic Club is second to none.

An albino conga - the blond leading the blond.

My daughter got a 3 Step Guide to Cross Stitch for Christmas, it didn't take too long for the anger to surface.

Polygami : Origami only with polythene.

I had a Gamekeeper for years. It was a real nightmare getting Mousetrap off him.

It's odd, however I still get a buzz every time I go back to the apiary.

Hawkeye

John took on a different persona when he did DIY and had an explosive short fuse. He was the Jack of all tirades.

Has a rabbit ever pulled a magician out of a warren?

Ventriloquist union admits their hands are tied as members go on strike.

Had a row with a friend over the quality of my stamp collection. He tried to butter me up afterwards, but I told him philately will get him nowhere.

My brother was on the door at the National Spelling Competition. He said if I could spell nepotism, he would let me in for free.

The WI can be a pretty intimidating bunch at times and for God's sake, don't criticise their home-baking. Hell hath no fury like a woman's scones.

Looking forward to the new quiz show all about hatmaking: Who wants to be a milliner?

I'm having a fancy dress party at the weekend, and I was going to go as a Samurai warrior. Unfortunately, the shop has closed for refurbishments. Sword's Law I suppose.

The World Crossword champion sadly passes away. His burial plot will be 3 down and 4 across the cemetery.

I'm the absolute best at creating fires. I suppose you could say I'm a narsonist.

Looking forward to seeing Ouija at the cinema. Great that they're finally doing a film about Glasgow board games.

Sign on motorway, warns that Frustration causes accidents. True, but playing Buckaroo and Kerplunk is far more dangerous.

Was caught daydreaming thinking if I should sell my rare stamp collection. Penny black for my thoughts?

Told a fantastic and hilarious story about my textile night classes to my wife who was in stitches: it was a right knitting yarn.

Cluedo film turns to tragedy as audience member chokes to death on popcorn and hotdog combo. It was Kernel Mustard in the Cinema.

HOME

Joss

A recent survey has concluded that more people take days off in Looe than than any other British holiday destination.

Last night in bed I felt like I was trapped in a u-bend beneath a kitchen sink, however, I was fine in the morning - it turned out to be just another one of my pipe dreams.

Never judge a duvet by its cover.

Am I the only person who is confused by our need to have Stainless Steel cleaners?

That's the trouble with feather pillows, there's always a down side.

Decluttering is at the top of seven out of ten people's bucket lists in Scotland. I blame it on fortnightly bin collections.

I spent ages online yesterday trying to buy a new toaster, but in the end I just gave up, too many pop ups.

The number of pop ups on the Compare the Meercat website is now getting ridiculous.

100% new wool carpet - that must be lamb in it flooring?

Hawkeye

Have sackfuls of red dots to put out in my weekly textile recycling bag. I think Wednesday is our bindi.

With all this reduced plastic and more and more people reverting to hand lubricating products, soap companies must be rubbing their hands.

Some people were incandescent with rage when they were told their traditional light bulbs were being phased out in favour of LED ones.

The person who came up with the idea of covering their fireplace, would presumably be known as avant-fire garde.

LITERATURE

Joss

To err is humane.

If Laszlo Biro had written a novel I wonder what his pen name would have been.

At the moment I'm in the middle of reading this really great novel called the Eternal Moggie, I just can't put it down.

Initially, the use of acronyms was hugely unpopular.

If an old guy with a long beard and a stick walks up to you today and offers you an Orc, don't worry, it's simply a Tolkien gesture.

Today I was going to write you all a sonnet, however, I can't as I've just lost my poetic license.

If you're stuck for words, just state the oblivious.

If anyone out there ever comes across a Handbook on Palm Reading, please get in touch.

The Monocles of Cornea series, by C S Gaseous, featuring The Tiger, The Wizard & The Sideboard and The Hound and his Girl.

Sandpaper: The world's most popular work of friction.

Scottish Pub Quiz Question of the Week Q. Which one of The Three Musketeers spent most time on a Sunbed? A. The Dark Tanned Yin.

Hawkeye

JFK Rowling, the President of children's fiction.

An amalgam is just a mass of logical abbreviated merged words.

2 bees audition for a Shakespeare production; or was it 2 wasps?

New book reveals lighter side to some of the most feared leaders in history: Attila the Pun out now in paperback (not hard).

Books on 100 things to do before you die: wouldn't it be better to have a book on 100 brilliant places where to die? Kick the bucket list.

Hatred of Mankind. By Miss Ann Thropy.

MEDICAL

Joss

Childhood obesity - I personally blame it on feeder schools.

Cairopractor - an Egyptian back specialist.

I had an amazing dream last night that I was an incurable insomniac, and then, just when it got to the good bit, I woke up.

The most effective part of yo-yo dieting is walking the dog.

Strange, after many years without any trouble my Hoover, which has just turned thirteen, is suddenly playing up, ...guess that's just a teenage dirtbag for you.

Preclampsia - the feeling you get when you see your illegally parked car about to be towed away.

Speculation - is that wondering what your next pair of glasses are going to look like?

My dentist is to be honoured with a plaque mounted on the wall outside his surgery, amazingly, it seemingly took around six months to build up.

Probiotics allegedly make us feel better yet so do antibiotics - I don't get it?

Cardiology: the study of ladies knitwear.

The only way to achieve a perfectly toned body is to eat all your meals with a tuning fork.

May be one day they'll find a cure for Panacea."

In my first year in the army I fainted over 25 times, I suppose I shouldn't have been too surprised that I was asked to attend a Passing Out Parade.

I believe it was just after Beethoven was diagnosed with IBS that he produced his Third Movement.

Topology: The study of the Fiddler on the Roof.

So how, exactly, do they count pollen?

The hardest question my Doctor ever asked me was, "So Joss, how are you finding your disorientation?"

I guess it must have been at Yale that they first pioneered Keyhole Surgery.

I took a nasty knock to the head in India and ended up in a Kourma.

Alcoholism has now been officially classified as an alement.

I just can't abide people who have digits missing from their feet, it really turns my stomach. The Doctor advised me that I'm Lacktoes Intolerant.

If you feel like you are always getting bogged down in life's details, it's most likely that you are suffering from Granular Fever.

Midwifery: The most labour intensive job in the world.

Hawkeye

Howling to the moon makes you into a lunartic.

Narcolepsy, getting crabby whilst you're falling asleep.

Citronella, you shall go to the mothball.

I've not been sleeping very well recently and need to invest in a more inflated pillow. I think I'll buy an egonomic one.

I remember when I had amnesia.

So easy to lose your head when you're growing up and full of hormones. Watch out for the guilloteen.

Nothing wrong with a bit of paranoia, as long as you don't worry about it.

I purchased an old van the other day which used to be a

mobile blood unit. It's not up to much but as long as it gets me from A to B negative, I'll be happy.

Sitting behind a booth with your hand up a puppet isn't my idea of exercise. The Paunch and Judy show indeed.

I got two centimetres taken off my nose recently. Is this Cosmetric surgery?

The coffee pot exploded on me the other day and has left me with a slightly percolated ear drum.

Although my wife suffers regularly from constipation, she never moans to me about it, and she usually gets something from the pharmacy which sorts it out. That's what lacks of tiffs can do for you.

I'm always spilling tea, coffee and beer over myself these days. I think I have Repetitive Stain Injury.

A doctor for the Paratroopers, said that his fear of flying, hopefully wouldn't interfere with his field work. Unfortunately, Para docs can sometimes have these problems.

I've decided to have a break before I go in for my hernia operation. My hiatus starts next week.

Don't be caught short. Pret-a-Potty.

I now have volunteered more than anyone else at the Sleep Behaviour Unit. You could say that I've slept my way to the top.

My Estate Agent keeps on swearing at me. I think he could have to lets syndrome.

Stupidly, I went out in the freezing cold wearing only a skimpy swimsuit and much to my partner's exasperation, I'm now in bed with mankini flu.

I know it's cornea, but eye love my optician.

Finance available on hair implant procedures. Check

website on how to pay.

Wearing an unwashed wig can give you a breakout of cold sores if you're not careful. Watch out for the hairpiece virus.

If you're going to commit suicide, but believe in reincarnation, you've got a dilemma on your hands.

Collected so much fluff in my bellybutton that I actually built a small submarine out of the stuff. I've gone all naval.

Envious of superior hand sanitising lotions. I'm well gel.

Insumnia is the inability to count sheep.

Broke my leg on the very first day skiing in the Pyrenees. I think I may have opened up an Andorra's box here.

The average number of people seen by my local podiatrist is usually 40 per day. Today it was only 15, even though he bravely came into work not feeling well. It was no mean feet.

Tried to sleep on a tempura mattress last night, but didn't sleep a wink. I felt completely battered this morning.

Lenzies: the place where people seem to see life a bit clearer.

Life's obituary, then you die.

Is an oncallogist available all the time?

If scientists can see DNA under the microscope in shades of only one colour, would that make it a monochromosome?

MUSIC

Joss

I understand that in the 1970s Meat Loaf's girlfriend used to often have one too many at their local bar and when Meat drove her home he got the inspiration for one of his greatest hits - "though it's cold and lonely in the deep dark night, I can see carrots diced by the dashboard light"

Jonny Rotten found in a large parcel yesterday. Another sad victim of the "post punk" phenomenon.

If band members of The Who went to prison the other inmates would be pleased as they'd finally have some mod cons

If listening in stereo is meant to provide a clearer sound why weren't we born with two mouths?

I hate people who harp on about stringed instruments.

I toured the world in a 1963 Nissan Dorma. Placebo

Domingo, The Fake Tenor

A recent survey has concluded that under performing orchestra leaders usually end up being sacked for gross misconduct.

What exactly, did we call stereotypes in the days before the introduction of the modern hi-fi system?

Albino music branded "white noise" by record label.

When Chopin struggled to come up with a new concerto, did he have to go back to the chopping board?

When I played in the brass section of the Royal Philharmonic, morale was so bad that the conductor had to force us to play Trumpet Voluntary.

Can a vocalist play an instrumental role in the success of an orchestra?

Florence Rida, what a guy.

22 11 12 World Sound Check Day

The Shows - Funfare for the Common Man

Albinos vote the Moody Blues song "A Whiter Shade of Pale" as their all time favourite.

Hawkeye

The death of REM: That's me in the coroner.

If Simply Red and Deacon Blue did a duet, I'm assuming it'd be a Deep Purple song they'd cover?

All Band Aid did was plaster over the cracks.

I got a new mandolin for my birthday a month ago. Already I've learnt 5 chords, two complete tunes and sliced 12 pounds of potatoes.

Aerosmith, Anthrax and All About Eve confirm The Nearly Alliteration Tour.

Vegetarian record collectors really love their Vinyl Leaves.

Could Pariah Carey be the ultimate diva outcast?

Has Jimmy Nail ever toured with MC Hammer?

You just can't take your eyes off these street dancers, they're so hiphopnotic.

Spandex Ballet. No need to worry about ripping your tights before winning Gold.

Surely the White album by the Beatles should be called the White ALBUMEN?

French operatic singer: Il fait Boe.

Robert Plant takes the escalator these days on his holidays. Stairway to Haven.

Black Friday is just a Blue Monday tribute act.

The X-cruciating factor.

Country legend's mom is making great strides in the jewellery world. Mother of Earle

Stevie Nicks on a life of no regrets: Je ne regrette Rhiannon.

If they lose any more members, they'll soon be known as, Take.

Town centre is absolutely dead this morning, even though there are the Specials on at most cafes and restaurants. It's like a ghost town.

By visiting the Sir Arthur Conan Doyle Centre, I didn't realise he initially liked AC/DC.

Been listening to The Killers a lot on my iPod recently. They sound like they're having a whale of a time.

DJs to go on strike in the run-up till Christmas. It's going to be the Winter of disco tent.

Amateur opera star and director of the local Inland Revenue office, Lesley Campbell, has claimed that sexism still exists in the workplace of modern Britain. She vowed to keep on fighting this prejudice as it ain't over 'til the

VAT lady sings.

Orkestrel manoeuvres in the dark - hunting for nocturnal prey.

Don't hear so much about Billy Idol these days. Loved his earlier career, but is it now Degeneration X?

Always wanted to see Rush on their onomatopoeia tour. I hear Squeeze used to support them.

Let me spell it out to all the fans going to see W.A.S.P and E.L.O on their joint acronym tour. Rumour has it that it's to be an abbreviated setlist. Better get my tickets ASAP though.

Strumming along whilst you're trying to clear mucus from your nasal passages - hair catarrh. Phlegming hell.

We all know Conan was a Barbarian, but how did his younger brother, Conun, learn to play the drums by himself? Now that really is a puzzle.

Looking forward to seeing ABBA on their Palindrome world tour.

The woman in my woodwind section can't take her eyes off me: she's getting very flauty

Got a feeling that Marc Bolan would have wanted to have left the EU too: T-Rexit

Fanta of the Opera : a story of a disfigured boy who finds love in an orangery.

The problem with Courtney Love was her terrible choice in see through underwear: it was her achilles hole.

I have a compulsion atm to put all my Bon Scott, Angus Young and Brian Johnston records in a particular order these days. I think I've got OC/DC.

Bruce Springsteen actually has his roots in Durban, Cape Town and Joburg. Born in the RSA.

They now have robotic dancing at the circus, can you believe it? Send in the clones.

I thought the Great Recession was a really poor magician?

Salt n Pepa have been going since 1985. You could say that they're seasoned pros.

Have dedicated a room to nothing but wooden sticks for my Afro-Cuban percussion project. It's my man clave.

Went to see Placebo once, and always thought it was a great gig. Looking back now though, did I really enjoy it?

Placedo Domingo had to resign due to alleged sexual harassment claims. His position became untenorable.

By having their two biggest hits, Anarchy in the UK and God Save the Queen, would the Sex Pistols not have been better off by just releasing Monarchy in The UK?

117 - MUSIC

NATURAL WORLD

Joss

Dinosaur Sale Now On - at T K Rex.

Forget dolphins, I spent this summer on the
beautiful beaches of Croatia and swam with Dalmations.

My pet pipistrelle is weird, he somersaults, balances on
telephone wires and often does head stands. I thought
this was odd and took him to the vet, she took one look at
him and said don't worry he's an acrobat.

Do all whales start off life as Pilot Whales?

With fly tipping at an unprecedented high,the word from
the dump is that many flies are now living like lords.

Can a Tapeworm tell exactly how much it has grown?

A wild goose chase - poultry in motion.

When polishing the car last week I couldn't help but wonder which part of a turtle could produce that much wax.

Stalagmites: Wee beasties found in German POW camp mattresses.

Yesterday I rubbed two stick insects together and made a firefly.

Mongosling: A Baby Mongoose.

Sorry, can't stop right now, I've got to see a manatee about a dogfish.

I'd love to see a fly poster featuring a giant picture of a fly.

Hawkeye

Yetis really are the absolute worst.

Fish sanctuary being very coy about where the new carp pond is going to be.

Lion gets hurt in mass brawl but says he's ok and all that's wounded is his pride.

The main difference between a naturalist area and a naturist area, is that one is a protected body, and the other is an unprotected body.

An owl tries to gain the love of a mate by telling them really funny jokes. It's a wit to woo tale.

Hamsters up in arms, as trade union talks goes full circle in favour of ferret wheels.

When those crocodiles and wolves get together for a counselling session, how can you believe a word of what they're saying?

Do bees ever suffer from hives?

In a naturalist coup, a Bald Eagle was seen flying over Wigtown yesterday.

The Black faced sheep is now so rare, it has become an endangered fleeces.

Of course, Blue whales use Sonar to help them communicate, but do they also have Blue Tooth?

A real mystery at my local RSPB club. I'm looking for a certain bird but false sightings keep throwing me off the scent. It's a red heron.

Horses are known for their huge genitalia. Have a thought though for the less endowed ones, full of embarrassment, standing all alone in a field in full view of everyone and trying to hide their smaller parts. They're the shire ones.

The humblebee is of course the most hardworking and selfless of the bee family.

Saw an authentic Scottish/Japanese carp fish the other day. It was the real McKoi.

OFFICE

Joss

360 degree feedback ... has it finally gone the full circle?

IT Team , we need the footprint for Project Yeti!

Instead of taking steps to escalate an issue, why not make life simple and take the escalator.

My boss asked me to collate a comprehensive report exploring how constant interruptions in the workplace affect productivity, oddly enough, I never managed to finish it.

We claim to live in a democratic society yet no one ever gets a vote when it comes to office politics.

Yesterday I overheard a colleague stating that he was "unindated with work". Presumably this means he's finally got through the backlog of paperwork he was previously struggling with?

It's only a matter of before chainsaw becomes a
new "buzz" word.

How do people deal with so many back to back face to
face meetings?

In the notes from a tribunal after my friend was
unfairly made redundant, they've brilliantly her by stating
that "she felt like she was being made the escaped goat."

Please don't shoot me, shoot the messenger.

He was like a kid in a china shop.

They suggest that there is transparency in our workplace,
but I can see right through it.

For a long time I thought that a crib sheet was just a
baby's blanket.

If you can't touch type, what, exactly, are the alternatives?

Has anyone seen the hidden agenda?

They were looking at ways to boost staff morale in our office, but they failed because the steering group lacked proper direction.

Let's have a heads up on Project Meerkat.

Hawkeye

I'm getting really fed up driving all my work colleagues to London, before they catch the Eurostar. So much that my wrists are aching. I think I've got car pool tunnel syndrome.

My boss was trying to explain the importance of finishing up a deal quickly and wanted some examples of a Summary Close. I said, would a bikini and a pair of trunks do?

The smooth talking, machine office guy thinks he's still got it, but times have simply moved on. He's known as the silver haired fax.

PETS

Joss

My unfortunate friend Albert Ross has always been dogged with bad luck, mind you his name has always hung heavy around his neck.

I once had a Mute Swan as a pet, but it wasn't much fun because I just couldn't get a cheep out of it.

Fair do's, it was definitely an albino pigeon.

How many young swans does it take to make a cygnet ring?

I found this sad note lying on the floor of the Canine Defence League offices yesterday.....Listen up Fido, don't worry about Spot, it's just the dog eat dog world of canine cannibalism. Your loyal friend Rover

If pigeons ruled the world, it would be a massive avian coo.

One of my kids brought back a tiny orphaned leveret for us to care for. They're much more demanding than a bunny, so much so, that the whole thing has proved to be a real hare raising experience.

That new canine postal service has proved to be a real dog send, especially for hounds in rural areas.

Is the Shire horse less forward than the Clydesdale?

My pet chimp has just passed his driving test in my 1936 Austin Martin, now he wants primate control!

Veterans of Crufts: The Toypoodle Martyrs

Hawkeye

If you want to know how far your cat walks in a day, then buy a petometer for it.

If I ever start up a dog walking and cat sitting business, I'm going to call it, Ca-t-nine lives.

Just bought a dog which is a cross between a collie and a labrador. It rounds up toilet rolls....One man and his bog.

French poodle having its lunch. Bone appetit.

My fluffy 12 week old kitten just did an adorable 45 degree somersault. It was a cute angle.

My dog is so picky with his food. He's a bone fido fusspot.

PHILOSOPHY

Joss

My alter ego is oge

Yesterday I was just thinking about going to the toilet, next thing I had a brain dump

For a number of years I grappled with the idea of retirement but in the end I just gave up.

Pathology: The study of walkways.

Tread warily, for every uneaten banana is a potential banana skin.

Gastronomy: Cooking Stars.

Anthology: The Study of Ants?

So Crates - "The philosophical packing and distribution company."

Mind Mapping: Compass Mentis.

Trilogy: The study of bird seed.

As we struggle through our lives, a woman becomes consumed by fear and self loathing, while for a man it always comes down to beer and self loving.

How many people do you know whose Grandmothers' spent any time whatsoever sucking eggs?

I was a Tyre Fitter for a spell, then one day I just jacked it all in.

I used to work in a Sauna, but in the end I threw in the towel.

Reverse psychology - backward thinking.

Brain dumps - crap ideas.

Hawkeye

I'm more of a glass ¼ full person.

Formica is temporary, glass is permanent.

People who feel sorry for themselves are a perfect example of the, Why always me, attitude at times. It's the e-pityme of selfishness.

One good automobile turn deserves another. So says my karmic-anic.

POLITICS

Joss

As a fervent supporter of the anti capitalist movement i always use lower case

Watch out – a revolutionary can turn you at any time.

Going round in circles can turn into revolution

Surely it doesn't take a G8 Summit to figure out that the best way to halt the rapid build up of damaging Greenhouse gases is simply to ban Greenhouses?

Whatever happened to Neon Trotsky, the leading light in Soviet Socialism?

Does free speech simply lead to cheap talk?

Mensheviks: Communists who didn't have the bols.

A conservative estimate puts the cost to the green economy of the last Labour government's liberal spending at £3 billion.

Hawkeye

Stop the EU leaving process now! Brakesit!

America set a dangerous precedent in giving Trump full power.

I don't really know what's been wrong with me over the past week. I keep on telling lies, filling in forms incorrectly, sweating and generally coming across as a hypocrite. I think it could be election fever.

William Hague's politics are just Double Dutch to me.

A Coup d'etat. A polite overthrow of a Government.

Brexitears.

No wonder the House of Lords causes such controversy. Imagine letting Peers Morgan in.

If a country was suddenly declared a Banana Republic, would this be classed as Topical fruit?

People were always trying to press Margaret Thatcher for an off the cuff straight answer. They didn't call her The Ironing Lady for nothing.

I can't make it to my polling station to vote in the Election, but you can apparently now vote via your Iphone. A case of Proxy Music

Sick to the back teeth of Brexit. First I wanted to Remain, then hearing other arguments, I definitely wanted to Leave. Now I'll just be so glad when it's all over. I'm now a Reliever.

RELATIONSHIPS

Joss

Coconuts washed up on the beaches of Tiree reminded me of a lonely hearts entry that I read recently..."lonely Hebridean Greengrocer seeks vegetarian female to share last mango in Harris"

Campanology : the study of tents.

Spotted this recently in the lonely hearts section of a Greek newspaper - Alpha male seeks Beta female to share Pi.

If Armitage Shanks were to wed Kimberly Clark, would it be a marriage of conveniences?

Hawkeye

If I had to describe myself in 3 words, it would have to be thick skinned, sensitive and contradictory.

Dorothy didn't appreciate the present that I got her for her birthday this year. I thought that it would look good next to the toaster, but it was a case of Dot recalling the kettle back.

Don't be downcast at being a virgin, celibate it instead.

Saw a bunch of Indian women having a great time on the eve of a wedding. It was a hin do.

Just broke up with my girlfriend who is a mosaic tile designer. She's in absolute pieces, I have to say.

RELIGION

Joss

My pet Chimpanzee, currently The Reverend Greystoke of Yarrow, looks set to become the next Primate of All England.

Chipmonk - a deep fat friar.

A promiscuous vicar in our area has been fired. The church deemed him to be a loose canon.

The Reverend Jim Henson : Pastor of Muppets.

Adam & Eve: The mother and father of all parents.

Tomorrow we'll study Monks' eating habits and take a long look at Peers.

Exactly how do Trappist Monks swear their vow of

silence?

I understand that Christianity as we know it today was originally kicked off by two blokes from Glasgow called Chris 'n' Dom.

What do you call Scottish followers of the Mennonite religion?..... Hamish

I hear that Hare Krishna has announced the name of his new born son. He's to be called Leveret.

Nuns: Birds of Pray.

Hawkeye

Atheists believe in the immaculate misconception.

Do they take their robes off at a Buddhist colony?

Russian priests versus Greek priests in a 5 aside football tournament? That's unorthodox....

Was driving at night time in the Jewish quarter recently and nearly knocked down a priest who just wandered onto the road. He was a rabbi caught in the headlights.

Do Celtic fans ever have sash windows?

Saw a Jamaican with blond hair the other day: the elusive Rastafairhairian.

Religious and sanctimonious? High and piety.

Pope fires unruly priest: he was simply a loose canon.

Do nuns wear pope socks under their habits?

SCIENCE

Joss

Fireworks manufacturing, it's not exactly rocket science is it?

So tell me, who on earth counts Geigers?

Even after the great alchemist, Ernest Rutherford, first split the atom back in the early 20th Century, he knew it wasn't quite the finished particle.

Every now and again I refer to the Periodic Table.

Just before the bulb was invented, you could always depend on its forerunner, the pilot light.

I read that there was something called a stereo telescope, is that not just binoculars then?

145 - SCIENCE

Hawkeye

How much exactly does a telegram weigh?

SCOTLAND

Joss

Never throw glasses in Stonehouse.

Hawkeye

Wabbit: A really tired Scotish bunny.

Rabbie Burns got an earful from his wife when he returned home from his Scottish tour. He was given the third degree.

Went back to my Mount Florida home where I was born and found the whole experience so uplifting. It was very Cathcartic.

Scottish misquotes: Bellahouston, we have a problem.

SOCIAL MEDIA

Joss

Did you know that the first thing ever to be Tweeted was The Birdie Song?

Hawkeye

Trying to set up this video communication platform that's all the rage just now, but am getting nowhere fast. What a zoomer.

Was just about to upload a video onto Youtube, when I started feeling unwell and began coughing and spluttering. I think it's the start of something. I bet you it's going to go viral.

People who constantly write online about their achievements are also known as blawggers.

Finally signed up to Tumblr. I'm a glass half empty kinda guy with these things though.

SPORT

Joss

Last Saturday I had a boxing match against a Heavyweight Campanologist - it was a ding dong battle for the first eight rounds but in the end he knocked ten bells out of me.

They tell me that at the Bookies odds can be evens, how even is that?

Outrage as Glasgow Rangers football club refuse to play fixtures in Orange Free State, South Africa.

Inn fighting continued last night as the Pig & Whistle defeated the Fox & Hound following a tight contest in Bradford. Tonight the White Swan takes on the Black Bull in Wigan where locals expect it to go the full fifteen rounds.

If Scotland ever manages to produce the best golfer in the world I reckon he'll probably be called Lion Irons.

I've just taken up No Kwan Do - it's the new martial art that's almost impossible to master.

Be careful, sport can be dangerous guys - I recently pulled at a Tug of War contest. Now I'm dating a lass who's dug in her heels and roped me into a long term relationship. As if that wasn't enough next year she hopes to tie the knot!

Our football club recently played a cup match against a team of builders' merchants, we won the home fixture 2-1, however, we ended up getting beat on aggregate.

The match that decided the German League title was a Teutonic battle.

As far as I'm concerned, those individuals who are foolish enough to get involved in Cage Fighting should be locked up and put behind bars.

For a number of years I was employed as a golf course designer; however I got fed up with it because my boss was always picking holes in my work.

Who's afraid of Virginia Wade?

At our local park, the inaugural football match in the Canine Defence Premier League, between the Isle of Dogs and Houndslow Town, had to be abandoned by the referee after only 20 minutes due to excessive fouling.

The match that decided the German League title was a Teutonic battle.

I wonder what size of shuttlecock they use at the Badminton Horse Trials?

Back in the late 70s I knew a guy at school who thought that footballer Cyril Regis was a cloud formation.

Strange how basketballs aren't made out of wicker?

Sparring Partner: someone who chums you to the corner shop.

I remember the days when the London Marathon was sponsored by Snickers.

Our Leisure Centre is so busy before work in the mornings, that it's a real bum fight to get into the showers.

Water Polo : so much easier when you use Sea Horses.

It's odd how we work out at leisure centres.

Odd that Polo shirts are the biggest selling sports shirt in the world, yet only a handful of people on this planet play Polo.

Point-to-point: Joined up horse racing.

I admire those Ladies Only gyms and spas for upholding the same traditions as some of our great golfers.

There was a real carnivore atmosphere at the big game last night when the British Lions took on Hull Tigers in the opening round of The Safari Cup.

Hawkeye

Sadly, the young talented lad in our local cricket team fell apart in his first match. Guess it's just the way the rookie crumbles.

Wonder if Jockeys' wages were furlonged during COVID?

I keep a logbook of all my mountain climbs. It's my Kilamountjournal.

I always hoped Man City would have signed Shane Long for them, so their midfield would have consisted of: Long, De Jong, Silva.

The snooker player with the best appetite is Ala Carter.

Rafa Nadal is quite simply the best potter I've ever seen. He's definitely the king of clay.

He gave his opponent too many openings in his first round match. It was a bad day at the orifice for him.

The hard of hearing World Cup has thrown up a nightmare group stage, involving Brazil, France and Spain. It's the ultimate group of deaf.

The Austrian tennis player, Dominic Thiem, disproves the theory that there's no I in team.

Massive German football phone hacking scandal comes to light. Leverkusen inquiry set up to investigate.

Jose Mourhino, the serial club manager. The Special K one.

After missing 4 birdie chances in a row, I admit that my behaviour wasn't what you'd expect to see on a golf course. That's what a Four Par does to you.

I was at Ascot at the weekend, and was surprised to see Horse D'Oeuvres on the menu.

Senior official for Catholic 5 aside football team receives warning about his overzealous tackling down the wings. He was given a Cardinal sin bin for 10 minutes.

If IKEA has a football team, do they play the flat pack 4 system?

Could Acronym Stanley be the longest football team name in the world?

Could Tiger Prawns win The Masters Chef again?

I wore plus fours the other day, but shot a 76 on a par 72 course.

I went to my Cricket Club dance the other night, but the bouncers wouldn't let me in.

Do you get Federer Special Agents in Switzerland?

I don't like our new Dutch defender, William De Bacle; he had a disastrous game on Saturday.

Although I like my George Foreman grill, I must say that I prefer my Ricky Hatton toaster

With Guardiola's tik-tak style, he's surely absolutely minted by now.

The actor, David Yip may be good at golf, but I wonder if his putting is up to scratch?

I think cricket teams' collective batting lack of concentration should be renamed, co-lapses.

The new German footballing superstar, Otto Emmune keeps on breaking down in training.

Juan Martin Del Potro's brother is called Rodney Potrotter.

It took a last minute goal to break the dreadlock in the Jamaica v Trinidad & Tobago football derby.

Thriller in Vanilla: Muhammad Ali's little known ice-cream shop in the Philippines.

Trying to teach your unruly dog to play cricket is certainly not easy. He knows no boundaries.

So Murray finally loses the nickname of unhandy Andy by winning his first major in 2012. I bet he was glad to get that moniker off his back.

Robin Van Persie got a special wedding invitation whilst on holiday with a friend driving round North America. So RVP got a RSVP as a VIP in a VR driving around VT.

Jerzy Janowicz has JJ on his socks. Why has he nicked Jelena Jankovic's socks?

Going in for this year's freediving competition, but not really done enough training, so as far as my chances go, I'm not holding my breath

I wonder if Gael Monfils supporters ever shout out, "Come on my son."

Johan almost changed his mind at the last minute before doing his famous backward flick. It would therefore have become known as the Cruyff U-turn.

Giving the ball to your opponent instead of a teammate is of course a faux pass.

David Beckham played in L.A and of course for Real Madrid. That makes him a Galaxyico.

If the 100 metres race is classed as the blue riband event, surely the discus is the wagon wheel event?

Roy Keane is A Chiles heel.

Barry Hawkins the professional snooker player works in a gift/gadget/puzzle/toy shop at the weekend. How bazaar.

It's very popular in Uruguay to go round to friends for a quick bite to eat at night. Soirees are part of their culture.

Kimiko Date-Krumm was a Japanese former pro tennis player who was so good that she was still playing at the age of 47. Her match ups against most of her younger opponents you could say was like menopause against boys.

Raheem may by his own admission in the early part of his career didn't always score enough goals away from home. It was a case of Sterling having a low conversion rate.

During Andy Murray's slam winning years, his pulse and bowels were so healthy and regular. It was surely the lentil effect.

Gareth Bale should really be playing in La Leeka.

As someone who doesn't really like American Football, I find the Superbowel a bit shit really.

Platini on hearing who kept their jobs as part of FIFA's shake-up: ' I can't believe it's not Blatter.'

Mo Salad: Cool as a cucumber!

163 - SPORT

STORIES

Hawkeye

I was in a rush as I squeezed into a hack. I had a good natter with the driver who had just won a flutter on the horses and was buzzing. He mumbled something about his breakfast: snap, crackle and pop, but there was a clap of thunder and a honk from another driver who we narrowly missed. Phew! We stopped suddenly and I gave the glass a good thud to see what was up. It's as if he was in his own bubble, so I knocked again and he told me to zip it. By this point he was having a bit of a sniff, then started to cry. Under new regulations he had to charge me the minimum fare, even though it was only a 2 minute ride. You see, he was on a meter payer!

I went for a job at my local pub, the 'Oxymoron', the other day. My car broke down but I got a lift from some Hells Angels. There was a still wind around so it wasn't too much of a bittersweet experience. When I got there, it was so quiet, it was like night of the living dead. It was a minor miracle they needed someone to work there. I eventually didn't get the job, but I was a wise fool to go anyway, and the owner said I definitely maybe had a chance the next time. It's almost limitless the number of times I've heard that.

My first exam that I sat was on punctuation. I was so nervous that I started to hyphen ventilate and made a dash for the toilet. I had a quick slash, composed myself, and returned to the exam. However, later at home, my colon began to hurt and thought I was having a stroke. I collapsed, pulled the brackets off the wall and was in a comma for a few days. There was a question mark whether I would pull through, but thankfully I did and also passed my exam. The results were a week late though, so they'll not be a post trophy for the Royal Mail.

My new optician is half Spanish and half Swiss. He was looking through his glasses manuel, telling me about his recent family reunion in Basel, whilst confirming what I knew: he told me I had Fawlty Fawlty vision and said si bill could be quite expensive.

The DVLA has just confirmed that it has authorised the longest personalised number plate in the world! Mr Peter Edward Robert Stephen Oliver Neil Alan Liam Ian Scott Eugene David Niall Uriah Mark Ben Eric Rory Paul Larry Alistair Toby Edwards, a long distance lorry driver, said he was very happy with
P.E.R.S.O.N.A.L.I.S.E.D.N.U.M.B.E.R.P.L.A.T.E.

Queuing in the Post Office the other day, I joined the 10

letters or less aisle. The checkout girl said, unfortunately Sir, you have misinterpreted the information that is specifically set out on the noticeboard in front of you. I'm sorry that you've miscalculated, but please join the queue counterclockwise.

Durex firm tries to think of short but catchy sounding name at January board meeting. Action Cock Rubber Organisation New Year Minutes.

Reading poems or looking at pictures with a hidden meaning can bring me out in a terrible rash. I think I have an allegory to them.

SELFIES. Or the full acronym: Selfish, egomaniacal, lordly, flaunting, inflated, egotistical, self-important person.

Scots-Indian matriarch gets penalised for bread theft, bolting from the crime scene and then claiming her husband shoved it down the loo....Major bread-fan Gran who ran, gets wan match ban, for nicking a nan, but who blamed her man for flushing it doon the pan. She escaped the can.

The famous triathlon competition, Ironman, has just finished, where athletes swim, cycle and run huge distances. I've just completed the lesser known Ironing Man competition where I was pipped to the title by a short collar and a pair of cuffs.

Manager of Composers football team get blasted for not getting a Handel on things. He was forever Chopin and changing formations, always on their Bachs and producing too many tactical Liszts. He admitted that his time there will soon un-Ravel.

SUPERNATURAL

Joss

Following reports that our local leisure centre is haunted, a Ghostbuster has been invited to set up a weekly Exorcise Class.

Vampire artists are just so predictable... they always end up drawing blood.

I was a Medium for years, until eventually I gave up the ghost.

Did werewolves used to be wolves?

Sadly, the future of our local Clairvoyant is no longer clear. A sign in her window reads "closed until further notice due to unforeseen circumstances".

Hawkeye

Satinism. You can't help but worship silk.

I know it sounds daft, but vampires do feel bad about drawing blood. They just get fangs of guilt now and then.

Went out with a New Zealand nymphomaniac, devil worshipper once. Naturally she had one thing etched on her mind. It was all six, six, six.

Just saw 100 men riding on 100 horses. I think it was a centaurpede.

TRAVEL

Joss

If the naked rambler decided to climb Mount Everest I suppose he'd be an expeditionist.

Are astronauts just highly trained Space Cadets?

An airport that was closed down due to sick building syndrome seemingly had a terminal condition.

I can't see space tourism ever taking off as no doubt the cost will always be astronomical.

To make it as a pilot you've simply got to have the right altitude.

Tentative: wary of sleeping under canvas.

I went to London to seek my fortune, however, just like

every other city in this country, all I found were streets paved with gum.

There was a nasty two vehicle collision last night on the M8 when Quasimodo bashed in to the car that the Elephant Man was driving. A spokesman for Strathclyde Police seemingly described it as a freak accident.

A colleague was telling me that he's just booked an exclusive luxury holiday in Saudi Arabia, then added it's in an All Inclusive resort, how odd.

If you travelled to the four corners of the globe, which places would you end up visiting?

If the Statue of Liberty is considered to be an iconic landmark, does that make the Eiffel Tower ironic?

Never accept a traveller's cheque from a Nomad.

Ex Pats: People who used to be Irish?

Now that they no longer have conductors on buses are they more prone to lightning strikes?

Mobile Homes: Anti Static Caravans.

Is anyone out there able to offer me any little clues as to how I get to the Hinterland, as I can't seem to find a map of the place anywhere?

You can never go on foot to Distraction.

The word on the street in Alva is that we're soon going to have a new vernacular railway.

I was gutted when my North American dream holiday in a tepee was over before it began, the lady at reception told me that I had to make a reservation first.

Seemingly the bloke who invented the reverse gear for the automobile didn't even have a backup plan.

Hawkeye

I was on holiday in Paignton and had the best salad I've ever tasted. It was pure dulux.

Qatar is an incredible country by all accounts. What snot to like about it?

My favourite tourist attraction in Britain, must be Madame Tussauds. I could wax lyrical about that all day.

Wandering around the souks on holiday in Morocco, trying to barter with the locals, was to be quite honest, all very bazaar.

My friend's just back from holiday and his hotel apparently had an awesome infinity pool. He went on and on and on and on and on about it.

Brighton, Skegness and Clevedon are constantly trying to keep up with Blackpool. I'd say it was just pier pressure.

The people of Dundee love to put little garden gnomes and dog ornaments along the side of the embankment. It's the River Twee.

Bought Exmoor, Dartmoor and Snowdonia national parks recently, albeit with a huge bit of controversy. Views are my own.

Absolutely delighted to have got rid of my mobile caravan. I'm ex-static.

Traipsed through the Amazon to spot the manakin bird, only to see it flying off in front of me. Missed it by a few seconds. What a dummy.

Was on a dancing holiday in Cardigan Bay when I was asked to pullover by a cop. He's just back from Jersey. He then asked shawl we dance?

Aboriginal family go walkabout on summer break. It's the original bushman's holiday.

My Venezuelan neighbours are completely bonkers. You

could say they're absolutely caracus.

Sagaluf:where OAPs zimmer the night away.

A survey out today will officially name the Greek island of Pathos as the world's saddest place.

The Hardknott and the Wrynose passes are notoriously steep roads to climb in the Lake District. I've always found the Hard-nose pass even scarier.

I was in Florida recently on holiday and went swimming with endorphins. I felt ecstatic.

If you're looking for a local railway, just ask some of the natives. They'll direct you to the vernacular one.

Contamination. Is this the world's deadliest country?

How many people with double-barrelled names go riding shotgun?

TV

Joss

As a child I loved the noise that the Clangers made, then strangely, this morning I woke up and wondered what sound they would make if you dropped one?

In the 1970s I always got mixed up between Roy Hudd with Rod Hull, but who would win a fight between those two?

The X Files: Science Friction.

I used to be an Avid Merrion fan, not quite so keen now though.

Seemingly Germaine Greer turned up in a large box at a Glasgow Sorting Office yesterday, yet another victim of the post feminist movement.

The biggest faux pas the BBC ever made was dropping the Clangers from their tea time slot.

Hawkeye

Some actors occasionally and unfairly get a reputation for possibly not always looking on the bright side of things. A case of negative equity?

Jamie to go on musical tour unaccompanied, doing Oliver: The Naked Clef

There's nothing actually wrong with the names, Thrower, Sugden and Jackson, per se.

Eric Morecambe would be so pleased at England winning the ashes. It's the return of little urn.

I really wish Alan Alda was a professional tennis player. That way, Hawkeye could challenge Hawkeye.

John Travolta has pulled out of filming for Grease 7 due to the Zuko virus.

At Marcel Marceau's funeral, there was a minute's silent

applause.

Will the King send himself a telegram if he reaches 100?

Imbecilic East Europeans to star in a new documentary about debauchery and general cluelessness : Georgia shore.

Celebrating the UK's birds of prey thriving population: Britain's got talons.

The 'hilarious' antics of a family run moisturising firm with slapstick swearing by the female CEO. Molton Brown's Boys.

As sad as it is to say goodbye to an old favourite, we have to move with the tynes. Auf Wiedersehen Peat.

My favourite TV programme is Misnomer Murders, but I'm always getting the murderer wrong.

Look good naked? Not always. The Gockit Wan.

It was a guilty pleasure on a Sunday night, but was Moniker Of the Glen, the real title?

I'd put brinery numbers into Room 101. Take that with a pinch of salt.

Miss Piggy keeps Kermit dangling. That would be a Muppet on a string.

Gran designs: bespoke housing for the elderly.

A woman on Embarrassing Bodies has complained of excessive bleeding and says sex is just out the window. Pretty dangerous position I'd say.

TV idea - The BBC wanted to sneak Peter Sallis in to commentate on the Open Golf's fashion, to replace Peter Alliss and call it, "The Wrong Golf Trousers".

New Scandinavian police drama coming soon on BBC4, centres around a curmudgeonly DI driving around in a Jag in beautiful countryside:Norse.

The Swedish chef really was the odd one out in The Muppets.He was the only bi-lingual one. Anomaly doo doo doo do do anomaly doo doo doo do.

Loving Africa just now: Attenborough's latest gem. Missed the last series on birds though. One of my biggest egrets.

He can kill quite easily with either his left or right hand. Ambidextererous.

Tim Wrath - the world's angriest actor.

Scooby Doo to bin burgers as Scooby snack and now only eats fish. Those pesci-tarian kids.

WORDS

Joss

Flamboyant: Something that's on fire but can float on water at the same time?

It was wrong with a capital R.

Quango - A dance for ducks.

What is the plural of a cappella?

Symmetry – The fine art of vest wearing.

Hawkeye

Deathly, unforgiving crowd at this month's Play on words, evening. You could hear a pun drop.

Arr! OMG Penis....Yep, that's Piers Morgan for you.

Bit windy tonight and going to see an outdoor production of Shakespeare. Just not sure if my wig will stay on or not. Toupee or not toupee, that is the question.

Donald Trump? An old turd MP.

They say eating a bit of chocolate is good for you. I've eaten so much Toblerone, I'm now a leen robot.

David 'Bumble' Lloyd's full name is, U Mild Odd Ball Bevy. A collection of eccentrics!

A Spoof Drill. Ya! There's always time for anagrams on the 1st of April.

Tess Daly can't have Sad style?

Should it not really be spelt, Alinement?

Trying to say red lorry, yellow lorry properly is classed as an articulated vehicle.

X-RATED

Joss

Nude freefall paratroopers - chute to thrill.

Is it true that Scotsmen wear nothing under their kilts or is it just a phallusy?

A missionary is in a difficult position as a nun he was working with claimed she was "surprised" from behind by him. Distraught Sister O'Daily hoped that he'd go down for a long time, however, in court the judge deferred sentence for a month.

Is there a height restriction for those wishing to join the Mile High Club?

Unprotected sex is potentially foetal.

An Asian penis expert was accused of taking a Japs eye view at a recent ejaculation semenar.

I heard a rumour yesterday that Madonna is proposing to launch her own range of condoms under the brand name "Immaculate Contraception".

Fornication on a kayak – canoodling.

Why do I feel oddly turned on just seeing a wild ox with big hair struggling to stay upright having just stepped off a playground roundabout? Hold on, I think I know why, ofcourse, it's an affrodizzyyak.

Condominium : a house in which to practice safe sex.

Extortionist seeks black male to rip off clothing.

I understand that a group of female scientists have managed to create the world's first test tube sperm, their male counterparts still remain baffled as to how they'd actually pulled it off.

I personally couldn't give a flying fuck about what goes on in the Mile High Club

Does the Wickerman have basketballs?

Last night I woke up to the sound of our two house ghosts having sex in the corner of the bedroom, the ghoulies were definitely out.Oh no I thought, not another phantom pregnancy!

Feastiality: a fetish for sex on a fully loaded banqueting table.

I once met a man so Albino that even his japs eye was red!

When you get involved in S&M you've really got to have your whips about you.

Overheard it on a bus in Glasgow.."I went tae the pictures last night." " Oh aye, what did ye see?" "A cannae mind the name o' it, but it was wan o' yon chick lick things." "Was it an 18 like?"

Hawkeye

The wonder contraceptive: The crotchless bra.

If you're unable to see things with the naked eye, then you could be a myopic naturist.

Seeing these huge, rotund male dancers dress up as women in the local am-dram musical, was a sight to see. It was almost burly-esque.

Not all Ethics girls have loose morals.

Two mathematicians living together and not even married? Must be living in sine.

Behind the massive spray, Viagra Falls is a very woody area.

I thought I'd seen everything sexually until Monique and Joan moved in. A mirage a trois.

TV idea: Great British Fake Off - where men try and spot if a woman is really, you know, enjoying herself...

Know an Australian who caught gonorrhoea. He was a right Jack the lad.

Scottish men are generally so crap at sex, there's even a book out explaining where they've gone wrong: The cannae sutra.

King Arthur was a prolific ejaculator. His castle was known as cumelot.

A warning to male Scottish tourists to Central America wanting to chat up local girls. The hawnd on your ass approach won't go down well.

Porn movie titles generally come out of the blue.

Went to an S & M garden centre today and bought a hose. Only thing was that it was full of kinks.

How was I to know the gunman had an imitation pistol when he raided the sperm bank where I make regular donations? I ended up firing blanks.

I support shouting and swearing at glossy magazines in its entirety... Profanity fair.

How much is that dogging in the window? Well it's free actually...

The CEO of a contraceptive company was forced by masked robbers to divulge his cashline number. He was said to have confessed under durex.

Baden-Powell's Be Prepared motto was more to do with not forgetting a packet of durex on an away trip.

There's a gorgeous new older mum who started working at the local ice-cream parlour recently. I wonder if a MILF-shake's out the question?

Ordered a woman's sex toy yesterday and I picked it up today. It was clit and collect.

Too many cocks spoilt the brothel.

BONUS MALAPHORS & OVERHEARD IN THE OFFICE QUOTES……..

You've really gone through the runner here.

Once I get my teeth into someone's trousers, I won't let go.

It would make sense for us just to piggy bank on their original plan.

It's like water off a dog's back.

This process will save us pinking e-mails back and forward.

We don't want this falling beneath the cracks.

Where did you clean that information from?

Look, just take solstice from the fact that this is the final run through before we go live.

Thanks for pulling the hat out of the bag on this one.

Last year we had a one size fits all approach, this year let's look for a much more generic solution.

We need to sort this out before the whole thing goes bear shaped.

Hilary managed to save this one from going into the net so now everything is doolally.

We need to pitch this right otherwise we're going to get dragged over the goals.

Sorry about this, but I'm going to light the blue litmus paper.

To hit our targets, I think we need to aim for a scattergun approach here.

I can only do bits & bats here.

I was only looking for a rough ballpark, but now we've been kicked into the long grass.

We have no option here other than to forge ahead with the Counterfeit Programme.

I think he's made a rod for his own bat now.

Not sure exactly where we are on this, but hey we are where we are, and at least going forward we know where we stand.

I think this particular swim lane requires a deep dive.

You've been through a whole gambit of emotions here.

We ain't got a bat out of hell's chance of delivering this before June.

I need to go back with some positive news, even if it's just to keep the monkey from the door.

We can turn the tap on & off here, but I don't want us to shoot our weakest child in the foot and later regret it.

It's like juggling spinning cats.

Now that we've concluded the initial fact hiding session, we can sweep the rest of this under the carpet.

We don't want you becoming a one trip pony.

I wonder if I could prick your brains for a few minutes.

You just need to stick to your buns on this.

It was so bad, I was made to feel like an escaped goat.

I'm not trying to wiggle out of this.

I'm sure we can take care of this in one fowl swoop.

This is a chicken and mouse situation.

This is a two way streak.

This is the bread and butter that we sink or swim against.

We need to adopt a one size fits all approach to Rightsizing.

Let's make sure that we are all swimming on the same wavelength.

We need to draw a line under the sand on this now.

Remember, Rome wasn't burnt in a day.

I think it's just the aurora I give off.

It's not rocket surgery we're talking about , it's a modern tossed salad!

We need to trunk up the elephant on this.

No one ever sees the chameleon in the room.

I reckon we need to open up the kimono here before the curtains come down.

The belt and braces have been left firmly round our ankles on this one.

We need a top down drains-up on this, with no holes barred.

Someone please show me the start of this end to end process.

I'm not really an extra large fan of t-shirt sizing.

This won't be an issue just as long as we are drowning in the same swim lane.

Someone's bouncing around on the phone out there.

This Heatmap's so red it's about to spontaneously combust!

There are two trains heading to the same tunnel here, and all I can see is a real car crash.

He's a key component in a spare part.

We're going to have to generically modify this process before it goes all bespoke on us.

Be careful here guys, we're playing a dangerous game of Russian Roulade.

Printed in Great Britain
by Amazon